Horses on the Farm

by Mari C. Schuh

Consulting Editor: Gail Saunders-Smith, Ph.D.

Consultant: Cary J. Trexler, Assistant Professor, Department of Agricultural Education and Studies, Iowa State University

Pebble Books

an imprint of Capstone Press
Mankato, Minnesota

Pebble Books are published by Capstone Press
151 Good Counsel Drive, P.O. Box 669, Mankato, Minnesota 56002
http://www.capstone-press.com

1 2 3 4 5 6 07 06 05 04 03 02

Library of Congress Cataloging-in-Publication Data
Schuh, Mari C., 1975–
      Horses on the farm / by Mari C. Schuh.
      p. cm.—(On the farm)
      Includes bibliographical references (p. 23) and index.
      Summary: Simple text and photographs present horses, how they are cared
for, and the work they do on ranches and farms.
      ISBN 0-7368-1189-3
      1. Horses—Juvenile literature. [1. Horses.] I. Title. II. Series.
SF302 .S37 2002
636.1—dc21   2001005345

Note to Parents and Teachers

The On the Farm series supports national science standards related to life science. This book describes and illustrates horses and their lives on the farm. The photographs support early readers in understanding the text. The repetition of words and phrases helps early readers learn new words. This book also introduces early readers to subject-specific vocabulary words, which are defined in the Words to Know section. Early readers may need assistance to read some words and to use the Table of Contents, Words to Know, Read More, Internet Sites, and Index/Word List sections of the book.

Table of Contents

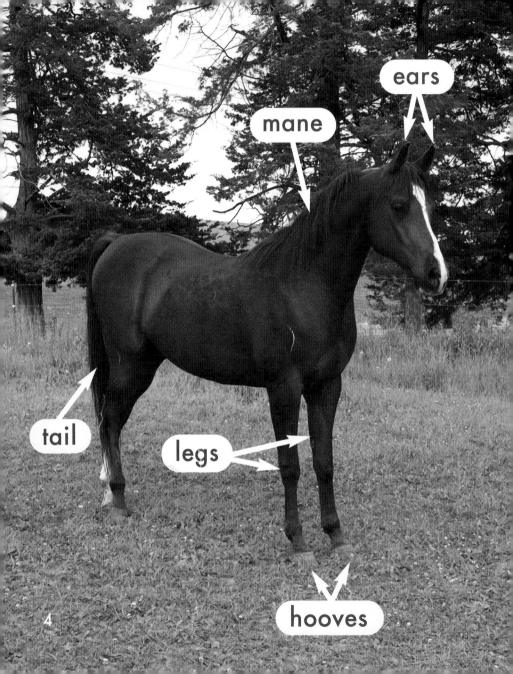

Some horses live on
farms and ranches.

stallion

mare with foal

6

A stallion is a male horse. A mare is a female horse. A young horse is a foal.

Horses are strong animals.
They have long legs that
help them walk, trot,
and gallop.

10

Some ranchers ride
horses to herd livestock.
Some farmers ride horses
for fun.

Some farmers use horses to pull plows and wagons. Farmers also raise horses for racing.

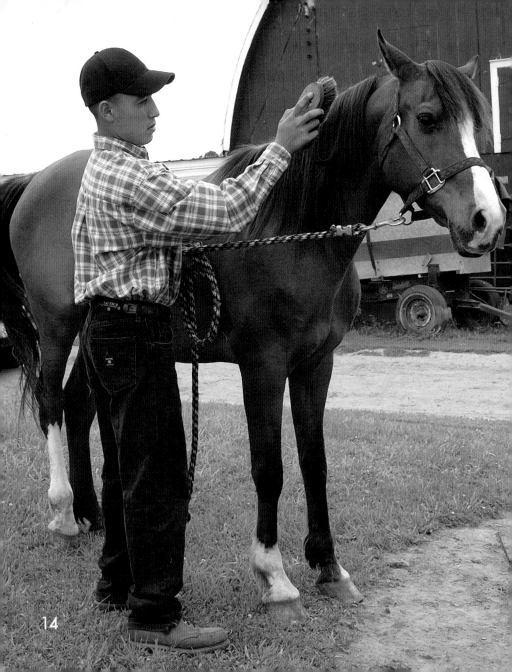

Farmers and ranchers groom their horses. They brush their horses and keep them clean.

Horses graze in pastures when the weather is warm. Some horses live in barns when the weather is cold.

Horses need food and water. They eat hay and grass. They also eat oats, barley, and corn.

Horses neigh.

Words to Know

barley—a common type of grain; grains are the seeds of a cereal plant; horses eat grains such as corn and barley.

gallop—to run fast

herd—to gather animals together in a group; ranchers use horses and dogs to herd cattle and sheep.

livestock—animals raised on a farm or a ranch

neigh—to make a long, high-pitched sound

pasture—land where animals can eat grass and other plants

raise—to care for animals as they grow and become older; some farmers raise horses for work or racing; other people raise horses to ride for fun.

trot—to move at a quick pace; trotting is faster than walking but slower than galloping.

Read More

Bell, Rachael. *Horses.* Farm Animals. Chicago: Heinemann Library, 2000.

Butterfield, Moira. *Horse.* Who Am I? Mankato, Minn.: Thameside Press, 2000.

Klingel, Cynthia Fitterer and Robert B. Noyed. *Horses: A Level Two Reader.* Wonder Books. Chanhassen, Minn.: Child's World, 2001.

Rustad, Martha E. H. *Horses.* All About Pets. Mankato, Minn.: Pebble Books, 2002.

Internet Sites

Breeds of Livestock: Horse Breeds
http://www.ansi.okstate.edu/breeds/HORSES/

Horse
http://www.enchantedlearning.com/subjects/
mammals/horse/Horsecoloring.shtml

Horsefun:The Homepage for Horse Lovers
http://www.horsefun.com

Index/Word List

animals, 9	graze, 17	pull, 13
barley, 19	groom, 15	racing, 13
barns, 17	hay, 19	raise, 13
brush, 15	herd, 11	ranchers, 11, 15
corn, 19	legs, 9	ranches, 5
eat, 19	live, 5, 17	ride, 11
farmers, 11,	livestock, 11	stallion, 7
13, 15	long, 9	strong, 9
farms, 5	mare, 7	wagons, 13
foal, 7	neigh, 21	walk, 9
food, 19	oats, 19	water, 19
gallop, 9	pastures, 17	weather, 17
grass, 19	plows, 13	young, 7

Word Count: 120
Early-Intervention Level: 14

Credits

Heather Kindseth, cover designer; Heidi Meyer, production designer; Kimberly Danger and Deirdre Barton, photo researchers

Capstone Press/Gary Sundermeyer, cover, 1, 4, 6 (top), 10 (bottom), 14, 18, 20
DigitalVision, 10 (top)
Photo Network/Stephen L. Saks, 12 (top)
Unicorn Stock Photos/Chuck Schmeiser, 6 (bottom)
Visuals Unlimited/Steve Strickland, 8; Joe McDonald, 12 (bottom); Inga Spence, 16

Pebble Books thanks Jeanne Zwart of Elysian, Minnesota, for her assistance with this book.